Love Story in Braille

By

Joe Quinn

Front Cover photography by Amanda Piercy

Front Cover model: Amanda Piercy

ISBN: 978-0-6152-1512-9

"murmur"

your heart
is a lighthouse
inside you

waves
waves
waves

all goodbyes

I'd like
to say
hello

"city lights"

you smile
like the lights
of a thousand cities

conscious
self-conscious
subconscious

that if the smile falters
the lights will go out
the world will fall apart

conscious
self-conscious
subconscious

that the weight
is on your back
and it's not at all like wings

"hotel room alone"

there is no sound
but the failure of the night
to bring a smile
to a quiet face

there is no touch
but unsure hands
parting thick curtains
like morning warm thighs

there is no rain
but god there should be
it makes falling appear beautiful
it makes the stars shy

"that legendary divorce"

summer in America
the land of milk and
honey not tonight
I have a headache
and I hate you
and I can't put it into words
but one small push
like kids on a swing
thinking that they can touch the sky and I
might kill you
for making me forget
what love is
or is supposed to be
or that I even want it

"in sects"

remember
when they broke your back?
and still you sang
rubbing your legs together

katydid
and so did everyone else

and we didn't feel
so small
hearing that music
as we walked away

katydid
and so did everyone else

"casualty"

we were pretty close
you were pretty
and I was close

this town wanted you
but so did I
I thought I was stronger
I thought you were stronger
inside
we were soft as fruit

this town ate you alive
I swear to god
I didn't tell anyone
how you tasted
inside
you were sweet as fruit

we were pretty close
you were so pretty
and some nights I was close

"coma/new car smell"

I saw you
get in the car
sunlight on metal
heaven's hair

I saw your face
through the glass
smile like a photograph
your eyes said "take me"

I saw you
get in the car wreck
sunlight on metal
heaven's hair

I saw your face
through the glass
frozen like a photograph
your eyes said "take me"

"anti-hero"

in the end
hamlet died

in the end
holden caulfield was just a boy

in the end
mexico ate dean moriarty and sal paradise

in the end
carlo marx wrote his poems in the dark
a pen in his hand
and a needle in his arm

in the end
james dean never found a cause

"miss xanax"

She says
"you don't have to watch"
As she gets things ready

Cellophane wrapper from a cigarette pack
A lighter
A cut straw
The pills

She says
"you don't have to watch
But I need to do this"

Takes the pills
Places them on the glass top table
Places the cellophane wrapper over them
Slides the lighter in slight crunches
The pale pink pills turn to dust

She says
"you're not going to cry are you?"

She takes an ID in which she's smiling
Says she's an organ donor
But she won't give me her heart

The card cuts lines
Leaves trails of thin dust behind
Dirty honey hair hangs down to the glass
And the straw jerks moving slow and then fast

She says
"you're not going to cry are you?"
I lie to her for the first time

"run if they let you/to me if you want to"

we are broken
-trusts
awash in tears
and cold flakes of rust
pick up the pieces
like phones when no one's calling
come together
falling
into arms
to arms
a war against
loneliness

"louisa"

I bet you're beautiful
before the mirror wakes up
before the sun fills its silver cup

what do you have up your sleeve
besides a bruise?
where would you be if you could choose?

and the hands move
mechanically
to apply make-up and remove sleep

and eyeshadow implies
some light from inside
and something in its way

(the days start like cars
in this parking lot life
we cough and crawl off
towards some distant light
and the cold smoke just hangs in the air
daring anyone half awake to attempt to care)

what do you have up your sleeve
but a bruise
baby where would you be if you could choose?

I bet you're beautiful
before the mirror wakes up

"it's alright(she was a young american)"

she got on a bus this morning
sun like rust on the horizon
I know someone was crying
over a girl like her not long ago

and this desert life's
just a dull knife asleep on the wrists
all the sharpness crept
into the words that inflict
the hurt of living like this

"you know I love you"
it flickers but the candle can't hold
"you know I love you"
it flickers and the firecracker explodes
"you know I love you"
god I've heard the words
so many times
they've lost all meaning

"anne frank, homecoming queen"

now that we're here
in the place we fear the most
lacking the voice
to ever call this home

we're whispers in the mouth of the door
we hide inside the walls
they're coming in...
I'll hold your hand

and the world
the world is a photograph
and the world
the world is under glass

and she knows where nothing is
the broken geometry of her star
and we know where nothing is
it rips the hearts from greeting cards
(we'll use the words they waste
as long as we have them)

and the world
the world is a photograph
and the world
the world is under glass

we hide inside the walls
they're coming in...
I'll hold your hand
we're butterflies and the door is ajar

"couldn't say a son"

I still say the same thing
just in a different way
"you're going to die in this town"
from angry 18 and damning
to a lonely quarter century
of almost understanding

(I'll feel sorry for you
your hands don't seem to know how)

are you getting all Jesus on me?
he asks

no,
they all get Jesus
they nail their feet to the ground

me
I want to be an angel
even if I have to paint a sky across this ceiling
and keep on climbing the walls

"run trip and fall"

love is a dead end
but there are houses we can stay in
long since abandoned
half candles on the windowsills

we were teenagers
on the front pages
of yellowing newspapers

were you holding a trophy?
were you holding a sign?
were you holding your own?
I was holding mine
you were in my arms

soul clot
so soft
we stop the life
from going to the brain

yes we were beautiful
some days no one remembers
yes we were beautiful
yes we were soft

"goodbye afterglow"

lonely nights
have the voice of stevie nicks
yes I know
that makes no fucking sense

the dashboard lights
come cresting over me
lit up like an astronaut
in a sci-fi movie from 1963

the radio calls
too far away to answer
the headlights reach
just to push away

so long afterglow
it's nice to know you noticed me
but I think it's time to be alone again

and if I come back
I won't be an insect
I'll be the hero that saves you

"vaudeville"

I am nothing special

just an old hotel
in which setting sun celebrities have died
in rooms whose numbers coincide
with something of significance
to someone at sometime

and some rooms
look down on parks
and some rooms
look up at stars

and on the sills of some
suicidal flowers just want attention
as you walk the surrounding blocks
their colors paint by numbers

and when you're inside me
(as you always are)
thoughts smile at you in the halls
soft voices say hello

and most nights
I leave all the lights burning
no matter the emptiness
no matter the cost

"conversations kill"

you stare at me
for the life of a cigarette
looking for words
you might not regret
burning
down
your doll house life

and life goes on
slowly
in all the wrong directions

you scream at me
the life of a cigarette
ugly words
some night you might regret
burning
down
your doll house life

and life goes on
painfully
in all the wrong directions

"somebody loves you wherever you are"

so many people in this life
are running around the ground floor
walls the color of dirt
chasing lights while theirs burn out

but you
you're on the roof
crying

when you cry
I hear a symphony of broken glass
like suicidal windchimes

when you cry
the starlight blurs into pearl ropes
hanging down to your shaking hands

when you cry
I want to hold you inside
like a second heart
a second chance at life

"my name is pill"

the kitchen is grey
a silent ghost
of a lifetime of spiderwebs

a woman sits smoking at the kitchen table
she's a good mother
never dropped a baby
she's a good american
never dropped a cigarette

though she doesn't know
her daughter has run away from home
she didn't leave any messages
in her Alpha-Bits
(teeth smeared with colored marshmallows)
there were only Cheerios
and screaming gets so old
just like kids

"my name is Pill
I know that's hard to swallow
but they said I was all
my mother ever wanted"

suicide notes cry for editing
smearing the ink to shades of bruise

the woman sits at the table
grey as the ghosts of cigarettes
watching the pointless life of ants
the linoleum their home
traveling the aqueducts of the cracks
the tiles placed too far apart
the gaps trip children
so the floor can then listen to their hearts

"have you ever been on the ground
breathing so hard
the force of your lungs
pushes the world away?

suicide notes cry for editing
smearing the ink to shades of bruise

"portrait of a girl, drying"

she leans on the pharmacy counter
like she's posing
for a painting
no one would buy

hair color, dusty,
like books she read
in rooms locked
to all but sunlight

thick rings on thin fingers
bone white
nervous, tapping
dreaming of a cigarette

eyes still alive
or even more so
but youth is slamming doors
up and down her body

on the shelf behind her
they sell artificial tears
I question the necessity
I question the validity

"since you left town"

I've had it up to here
it's a two story house
opened the window
and climbed out on the roof
of my mouth
screaming
and the sky is dying red
back of the throat trying
to take back what was said
and what was sad
was the way the stars
were laid out like broken glass
you broke into the sky
and what's left?
what did you take
besides a chance?
why didn't you take me with you?

"there are no beautiful men"

there are no beautiful men

just sweet boys
lost in the shadows
their light throws
black as funeral clothes
ten times too large
small and naked inside
with flowers for eyes
and hearts that pine

there are no beautiful men

"I am 1 a.m."

1 a.m. and I am
not asleep
not alive
walking a line
as fine as a hair
up to an angel's ear

1 a.m. and I am
painting flower fossils
on the cold glass
with my breath
your fingerprints are still here
holding the flowers

"alibi(a lullaby)"

head in the clouds
counting the rain
Emily don't you complain
move how you want to move
the world won't stop spinning
do what you want to do
the room won't stop spinning

we've been over this before
it isn't new ground
it's my heart

one foot in the grave
counting the flowers
Emily don't you turn so sour
blame who you want to blame
the world won't stop spinning
but it's the same all the same
the room won't stop spinning

hands in the clouds
painting the rain
Emily can't you see I'm in pain?

but we've been over this a million times
it isn't new ground
it's just my heart

"I was a teenage Jesus"

god bless us all
broken dolls
second hand angels
similes for stars

we're carpenters
we put up walls

nail down what they'd take away
nail down what they'd take away

"village of the damned"

a mob has gathered
Frankenstein faces
in the lights of torches
there is talk
of killing loneliness

empty houses
stand at their backs
long hallways
branching off like lungs
waiting to take in smoke

there is talk
of killing loneliness

"dream police"

the kids are in the dirt
the kids are into cutting
the kids are all just worms
making themselves smaller

hoping something will get away
why do we come out in the rain?
what exactly did we think we had saved?

the dream police are coming
giant flashbulbs mounted
to the roofs of their cars
taking pictures as a voice screams
through a bullhorn

repeating
"this is reality
open your fucking eyes"

"this world dissects angels"

she writes "cage"
all over her skin
she's naked
and afraid
of being clean and free

tossing in her sleep
hair stuck to sweat
black lines on white skin
a map of the places
they've taken away from her

she rips the pillows open
looking for feathers
she burns the house down
looking for the sky

"feral/fetal"

whose indifference
broke your back?

I remember
when you were six and dusty blonde
playing in the gravel
quiet and alone

before the days started pulling teeth
before the days started pushing back

whose indifference
broke your back?
you replaced your spine
with a shotgun

you're yellow
jaundiced
look at what you've done

kids spread like snow angels

you got a cheerleader
by the bathrooms
the quarterback
in the lobby

and you shot me
and Julio
down by the schoolyard

we were running like sweat
when the skin of the day turned cold

"rebel without an audience"

he keeps his cigarettes
rolled up in the sleeve
of his t-shirt
like the 1950's

he doesn't know the 1950's
he doesn't give a fuck
about the 1950's

but he keeps his cigarette pack
rolled up tight in the sleeve
of his black t-shirt
a placeholder for a heart

and he stands there
hair greased
but the machines won't run

he stands tall
the last brick wall
in a falling down building
condemned

"1993"

it's summer
it always is
a picture on a calendar

you're low
lying in the scent of high grass
and some animal part
has scratched out the word "sky"
and there is only space
stars asleep beneath this blue blanket
you could reach
and pull it up like the page of a calendar

but you don't
this month is hard to let go
there are days circled in hearts
in different colors of ink

and you're high
lying in the summer grass
sunlight like honey in the grain

"full blown youth"

god I've got to get away from here
there's too many people
dead inside their dirty lives
we're running out of flowers

and god is a beautiful girl
lips like the wet skin of sweet fruit
and heaven is whatever she says
should she ever speak to you

and I was born to run
I've studied the tears and rain
and a little boy's nose wiped on the worn clothes
of a long handed down pain

god I've got to get away from here
there's too many people
dead inside their dirty lives
we're running out of flowers

and god is a beautiful girl
lips like the wet skin of sweet fruit
and heaven is whatever she says
when she takes your hand and speaks to you

"young love"

he wears a jacket
the color of trees
inside he's
shaking like leaves
her arms are like swans' necks
everything is okay

dirty thoughts in the clean sun
smiling lips bee stung
she tastes like honey
and everything
is okay

"we don't have skeletons"

we don't have skeletons
we're flowers
stretched to obscenity

we don't have skeletons
we cower in closets
spineless on drunken nights

hey father
you're a mountain
hey father
you're a man now

"dust collects on light"

oh we're all so lonely
god if we could only
find someone to
find us out

we put on brave faces
work for slave wages
the days are just the same but
really was there ever any doubt?

mother's always crying
damn this broken record
the needle skips
the sewing never gets done

she says stop your praying
save your good jeans
a joke but it goes
right over our heads

oh the floor's so dirty
surely there'll be flowers
any day now

"there's a light(about you)"

even the pessimist
would say the moon is full
and fall in love with the way
the light falls on you
and you could have them believe
whatever you wanted
if you knew what you wanted

there are many things
of which I wish I could speak
but everything keeps falling
apart on me
and I told myself this time
I'd turn a new leaf
but on the back I just kept on writing

about you

"god loves my empty head"

cleanliness
is next to godliness
there are openings in heaven
for janitorial service

we can sweep the hallways
in our old age
we can climb chairs
when the lights need changed

did the light show you
what you wanted to see?
did you feel closer
to the sky?
did gravity pull your leg?
was it all a lie?

and I'm on my knees again
I swear I'll make this floor shine

"idlewild"

sixteen
and it's cool to hate your dad

save your tears for rainy days
and baby no one will ever know
that you're sad

but now that we've grown up a little
what do you see in the light of my halo?
why are they always looking down on me?

the park bench
is a landmark of sadness
it sits on the edge
of the forest

I almost made it
past the first line of trees
but you were there
waiting for me

and now that we've grown up a little
what do you see in the light of my halo?
why are you always so good to me?

"coal train"

in towns like this
the women only dance
across train tracks
swaying like an empty dress
drying in the summer grass

the train bridge runs
high above the river
and the transylvanian spires
of the telephone wires

are you picking this up?
the taped down stars
of flattened pennies?

are you picking up
this train of thought?

"the astronaut's suicide"

1.
"will you think of me?
when you're far away?"

don't I always?
the molecules say

we're all unwhole
we're all unholy
you smile when you see me
but you don't really know me

they sit beneath a tree
a string of pearls runs through the branches
pulled from the exposed throat
of a cold moon

"will you think of me
when you're far away?"

aren't I always?

2.
on the surface
he appears calm
the gravity slows movement
to a long perceived crawl

there's a radio in his chest
a lifetime of static coalesced
into a fetus

as he drifts
farther from them
they begin reciting
spoken word poetry to him

"come back come back
Major Tom come in
you severely risk the loss
of life and oxygen"

somewhere over the radio
he begins to sing
"somewhere over the rainbow"

on the surface
he appears calm

3.
did you see the video?
it's all over the news
the same looped footage
the same grainy views
(I think it's the dust in us
we're watching too close)

he walks to the horizon
becomes a dot
a period at the end
of an unread sentence

on the surface
he appears calm

"home"

home
is the body
holding me

home
is where
there are pictures of you
but no walls

home
is where
god lays his head
on my shoulder

home
is the body
I hold

"we hang ourselves, like calendars"

she never wakes up
but when her eyes are open
and her hands aren't busy
trying locked doors
she has cigarettes
for breakfast

he sleeps days
half naked on the floor
he cut a cross into the curtains
so the sun will shine through
burning the shape onto his back
if he were a vampire
it would kill him
twice
but somehow
he's never felt more alive

"funeral"

burgundy carpet
heads down
make-up runs
like wax from black candles

did you see the sunlight
coming in the window
when you said Father?
did you see the sunlight
when you spoke of His hands?

procession
turn on your bright lights
we centipede down the 11 a.m. highway
a black bird contrasts the blue sky
a smear of ink
a tattered rag
the last ash from a burning book

cemetery
patchy grass waiting for spring
plastic flowers waiting for what?
to be thrown away?

turn on your bright lights
and I shall not want

"the hum of naked electricity"

where there is smoke
there are black leather jackets
burning the world
a cigarette at a time

the sound of boot tips
striking low against
a chain link fence
and climbing
hands grip and push the stars
like piano keys
sing motherfucker sing

"family portrait in charcoal"

shoebox in the closet
photographs outlast
the borders undefended
the feelings come and go

don't touch it
you'll leave fingerprints
mazes for insects
miniscule ridicule
little laughter nailed
to the back of the throat

she leans over the box
paper doll small
cut from the transcripts
of lost conversations

her spine
the line of the bones
the finger touched bumps
of an old xylophone
the cold is home
in this elevator
stuck on the floor
with her heart

don't touch it
you'll leave fingerprints
mazes for insects
a cigarette glued
to a busted lip

"you"

you almost have
feathers in your hair
you almost have
heaven in your eyes
your life is all opening doors

I have you in places
I didn't know I had
you're inside my every thought and breath
like office space
you turn on lights and go to work

"she said"

you're going to end up
writing about me aren't you?
she said

I might
I might lie
put words in your mouth
instead of whatever else I had wanted
at one time or other

you're going to end up
getting hurt
she said

I told her I didn't care
that it'd be nothing new
just something more

you're not a beautiful man
you're just beautiful
she never said that....

but her voice was alive
with me
and that is what it said
to me

(you're going to end up getting hurt)

you're going to write about me
aren't you?

yes
and you'll be beautiful

"dead math"

I saw the best minds
of my generation…

…no I didn't

I saw a bunch of zeroes
waiting for a one
to stand in front of them
and make them something

I saw the loneliness
of clockwork
the sleeping teeth
locked into each other

the clock is broken
only right
twice a day

once
early in the morning
when they say
"something has to change"

and again
in the evening
"another day is gone"

"the city runs off"

the city runs off to the hospital
then a new city begins

migrant manholes
graffiti vandals with hearts of gold paint
stand out in relief in the headlights
(relief at finding something, anything)
caught in the act of science
shaking like the hands of funeral directors

the city runs off to the hospital
a bandage of fog burns off
in the early sun

the people on the corners
sell themselves short
heads down heading home
they walk right under the doors

"I like your shoes
but now how they walk away"

"I'm alive"
my nametag says
in the braille of gooseflesh

we eat what we catch
we are what we eat
we're cold and we're sick

the city runs off to the hospital

"kindling"

you sit on the porch
cigarette placed firmly between pale fingers
a lighthouse torn asunder
shining out to all the lost sailors
drifting under the sign of cancer

head down
fogged up glasses
the interior concave
so the tears collect
like medicine in a spoon
and you wonder
where are all the open mouths?

you cry your eyes out
but they stay inside your head
and you're forced to see

you fight sleep
like a schoolyard bully
swinging your fists widely and wildly
like a drunk dancing with ghosts
to swingtime songs no one knows cause no one wrote

and you wonder if life
could really be
as sad as a pyromaniac's wet dreams

"the king is dead and we're all forgiven"

american by death
the excess
a romanticized loneliness
he died on the throne
and expects us to extract
some message from the binary code
of cigarette burns across the colored carpet

the only difference
between a spotlight and a searchlight
is the occassion

nicotine stained linoleum
fingernails tap a scat staccato
body gripped in a fit of a seizure
a ragdoll shaken like so many hands
a paperdoll constructed of a lifetime of headlines
overlapped and gone black

the only difference
between a spotlight and a searchlight
is the number of people waiting to watch
the faces get caught
and whether or not they smile

"her eyes are sedatives"

some days
god is as sweet as a woman
blue skies
sun just like
a slice of lemon

an asylum of wildflowers
by the side of an empty road
always lost, but now in the scent
of someone coming
to take me home

and I know she'd listen
should I tell her of my burden
but instead I turn
and shut my mouth against
the curve of her neck

"james dean"

james dean went to california on a bus
stone face draped in the grease
of his hair, his mechanic's jacket
cigarette sucked tight to the lips
a nipple of an industrial age mother
then
Hawaii and Alaska were designated "distant America"
now
it's everywhere in between

beyond the outliers of light
we're spread as thin as patience
rural and gutteral
we cry wolf in this land of abandoned mirrors
we cry out
in warning and lament
as we all fall through the cracks

there was a girl
a failed christian in the way
she never blindly memorized every verse line for line
just the ones she believed
Victrola for a heart,
broken record on her sleeve,
a thin needle inside
tried to keep the lungs inflated
but it skipped, saying "love, love,love"

and she said to me
when I said to her
that we fell through the cracks

she said to me
yes
like sunlight through broken windows
warm orange pooled
on a dusty kitchen floor

"teenage radio"

said there's nothing wrong
with taking drugs
till it all went wrong
and they started taking us

see us now
as shells of ourselves
held against your ear
you hear the heart

sign off it's signal
sad static of a national anthem
the flag slides slowly
down its pole

said we're the kids
sick of the future
never been able to wake up
in no tomorrow

should I ever find myself
in such a place
I'm sure I'll be alone
and thinking of the past

"where is your fucking heart?"

I did the best I could
with what I had to lose
sometimes who you blame
is all you get to choose
fault lines, a sad state
everything nailed in place
we shake hands
so I know yours is empty
let go, I want to tear it down
please let me

such flowers in our arms
just to wind up at our feet
what children we are
just to end up on our knees
at least the ground is forgiving
but really
I don't think we did
anything wrong

"all her heroines are needle thin"

never been concerned
with the way you burn
just the places that you sleep

and I hope your heart keeps
on beating
whatever it is you're fighting

I'll be waiting for you
on the other side of this tired conversation
saying the same things I always do

no matter how many times I talk you down
you still get high
inward star you're nowhere near the sky

small town and no tall buildings
no sidewalks
heard your sister drew an angel in the chalk

and you laid down to stare at the sun
and let the beauty
make you blind

no matter how many times I pick you up
you still get low
small town and nowhere to go

but I've never been concerned
with the way you burn
just the places that you sleep

and I hope your heart keeps
on beating
whatever it is you're fighting

and I'll be waiting for you
on the other side of this tired conversation
saying the same things I always do

"hayseed"

all the burnouts flare out
just short of the bridge
but the town will forgive
all those lonely kids...

screaming out
in frustration
bleeding out
on nicotine stained pages
and your pen looks red
in the light of yet another cigarette

settle down your machines
and fall into line
you'll never cross this heart again
you'll never be mine

and I'm going to leave
he says
she watches him turn
he smiles
her eyes like a camera
she captures
the flag of his waving hand

"leaving the city"

you crook your arm
in the broken light
of the back seat
the shadow is a bridge
I sleep under

did we get away?
did we find a way?

I can see the coplights reaching in
caged fireworks screaming out

whisper to me
the dead men's names
of every street we pass